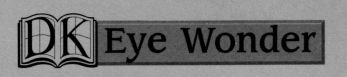

DK Eye Wonder

Horse

LONDON, NEW YORK,
MELBOURNE, MUNICH, and DELHI

Written and edited by Caroline Stamps
U.S. editor Margaret Parrish
Design coordinators Gemma Fletcher and Hedi Hunter
Picture researcher Ria Jones
Production Siu Chan
Jacket designer Natalie Godwin
Category publisher Mary Ling
Art director Rachael Foster

DK DELHI
Senior designer Malavika Talukder
Designers Neha Ahuja, Devika Dwarkadas
Production manager Pankaj Sharma
Senior DTP designer Harish Aggarwal
DTP designer Preetam Singh
Head of publishing Aparna Sharma

Consultant Margaret Linington-Payne, Director of Standards at the British Horse Society

First published in the United States in 2010 by
DK Publishing
375 Hudson Street, New York, New York 10014

Copyright © 2010 Dorling Kindersley Limited

11 12 13 14 10 9 8 7 6 5 4 3
008-175929-Mar/10

A catalog record for this book is available from the Library of Congress.

ISBN 978-0-7566-5854-0 (Hardcover)
ISBN 978-0-7566-5856-4 (Library Binding)

Color reproduction by Colourscan, Singapore
Manufactured in the USA by Worzalla

Discover more at
www.dk.com

Contents

What is a horse?

A horse is a mammal with extraordinarily well-developed senses that keep it on constant alert to real or imagined danger. Horses come in an amazing variety of sizes and colors, but all share the same basic features.

That's a good one!
When people say a horse has good conformation, they mean it has good bone structure, with its body parts in perfect proportion.

The horse we see today has evolved over some 60 million years.

Loins

Withers

Tail

Hock

Stifle

Sorrel

4

Beneath the surface

A horse's skeleton has 205 bones. Like all mammals, it has a backbone, and seven neck vertebrae But it has no collarbone (a feature common in mammals that run!).

Vertebrae

Skull

Neck vertebra

Point of shoulder joint

Ribs

Point of hock

The foot bones end in a single toe, protected by a hoof.

Mane

Poll

Point of shoulder

Muzzle

A horse has no muscle tissue below the knees.

The German Schleswiger is a heavy horse.

Shetland pony

How many?

From the Akhal-Teke to the Welsh cob, there are more than 250 breeds of horse worldwide. These can be divided into three main types: heavy horses, light horses, and ponies.

A bit about teeth

Horses are herbivores. They graze for about 20 hours a day, and their teeth are therefore made for biting, cutting, and grinding plant matter. A foal's first baby teeth are replaced by about 40 adult teeth, which age with the horse.

4–5 years

9–10 years

Close encounter

Skewbald, dapple gray, piebald, 14 hands, 12.2 hh… horses are often referred to by their color and size. Many people have a favorite color, although color does not affect a horse's performance or its temperament.

Ideally, measure by facing the horse's tail

A question of color

Horses are unusual among mammals for the range of colors in their coats. That range is a result of breeding particular horses together over hundreds of years. Here is a selection of the recognized colors.

Measuring up

Horses and ponies are measured in hands high (hh) or in inches or centimeters, from the ground to the highest point of the withers. A hand is 4 in (10 cm).

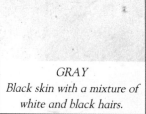

PALOMINO
Gold coat with white mane and tail.

GRAY
Black skin with a mixture of white and black hairs.

BAY
Brown coat with black mane, tail, and lower limbs.

BLUE ROAN
Black body with white hairs.

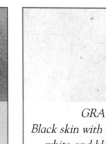

FLEABITTEN
Gray coat speckled with sorrel or black.

SORREL
Pale to rich red. Shades of gold with same color mane.

BROWN
Mixed black and brown coat.

PIEBALD
Patches of white and black.

SKEWBALD
Patches of white on a brown base.

DAPPLE GRAY
Dark gray hairs form rings on a gray base.

BLACK
Black with occasional white marks.

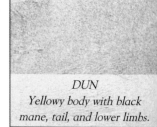

DUN
Yellowy body with black mane, tail, and lower limbs.

My horse has a star!

Many horses have white hair on their faces and legs, which makes a distinctive pattern. These markings have names.

This horse has a blaze.

STRIPE
A narrow white strip that runs down the face.

STAR
An irregular shape set between or above the eyes.

BLAZE
A wide white strip that runs down the face.

This coat is sorrel.

CORONET
White markings at the base of the foot.

SOCK
White markings to the lower foot.

STOCKING
White markings up to the knee or hock.

Movement

From a slow-paced walk to an exhilarating gallop... a horse's movement is called a gait. A horse has four natural gaits, each with an audible set of footfalls, or beats.

Walk

The slowest gait has four beats. While walking, the horse has two or three of its four hooves on the ground at any time.

Trot

This two-beat gait sees the right hind leg and the left fore leg move together and the left hind and right fore move together.

Canter

The canter has three beats: the left hind leg, then the left fore and the right hind together, and then the right fore leg.

Gallop

This is the fastest movement, with four beats. All four feet are off the ground at once for longer than they are in a canter.

The fastest a horse has been known to gallop is 43 mph (69 kph).

The fifth gait

A few breeds of horse have a fifth gait. The Icelandic Horse can tölt. A tölt is smooth to ride, falling between a trot and a canter.

The Pace

Some Icelandic Horses are able to do a "flying" pace. For this, the legs on each side of the horse move together. All four leave the ground at one point. It's a fast gait!

Speed kings

A galloping horse can typically reach speeds of 30 mph (50 kph). Horses cannot gallop for long, since a gallop requires a lot of energy.

Talking horse

Horses are social animals and prefer to live in groups. They communicate, or "talk," through body language and by using their sight, hearing, and smell to recognize one another and find out what's going on.

What good sight!

A horse's vision is excellent. It's very different from our vision though, because a horse's eyes are on the sides of its head. Horses can see almost 360 degrees, as shown by this diagram.

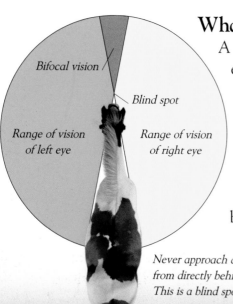

Bifocal vision

Blind spot

Range of vision of left eye

Range of vision of right eye

Never approach a horse from directly behind. This is a blind spot.

Listen up!

Horses also use sound to "talk." They squeal in aggression, or whinny with excitement. A mare will whicker (neigh softly) to her foal, while a stabled horse will whinny loudly if its meal is late.

Flexi ears

A horse has exceptionally good hearing. Each ear is controlled by 13 pairs of muscles, making it amazingly mobile. The position of the ears tells a lot about the mood of the horse.

This horse is showing fear or anger.

This horse is alert and responsive.

This horse is listening and relaxed.

Mutual grooming

Horses have favorite friends, just like us! They will stand with a friend, grooming that horse with a nibbling of their teeth on the neck and shoulder. Standing like this, they are also more secure, because they can keep an eye on each other's blind spot.

Some horses will use their back or fore legs to kick out at a perceived threat.

Get out of my space!
Sometimes it's easy to read a horse's intention. This horse may have been surprised by something behind it, or may just be asserting its status over a rival who has grazed too close.

What's that smell?
If a horse encounters an unusual smell, it will lift its top lip and "smell" with the sensitive membranes inside the lips, as well as smelling through its nostrils. This behavior is called flehmen.

11

Foaling

Foals are born fast: the whole process takes less than an hour, unless there is a problem. Why is it so quick? Horses are instinctively wary of being caught by a predator, so they need to be up and ready to go as soon as possible.

Pregnancy

Mares carry a foal for just over 11 months. Once the mare is ready to give birth, she will become very restless, lying down, getting up, and nudging her stomach area.

After-birth care

Foals are usually born at night because that's when the mare feels safest. After giving birth, a mare will remove the birth sac by licking the foal. This helps to improve the foal's circulation and breathing and strengthens the bond between the two.

The mare's teats are between her hind legs.

Look, mom!

A foal will take its first steps just 30 minutes after birth and can trot and even gallop when just two hours old.

HOW LONG CAN A HORSE LIVE?

The record for the world's oldest horse goes to a horse born in 1760 and known as Old Billy. He lived for an amazing 62 years and worked as a barge horse in Lancashire, England. Old Billy was said to be black with a white blaze on his head. His death was recorded in November 1822.

A female foal is known as a filly. A male is a colt.

Time to suckle

Foals suckle the mare for the first few months of life, gradually moving over to grazing. In the wild, they suckle for around a year, but domestic horses are weaned from their mother's milk after about five months.

Time to rest

Foals need a lot of rest: they actually spend about 12 hours a day asleep (but this is done in short bursts and not in one long stretch like humans). They usually sleep lying down, while adult horses tend to sleep standing up.

Horses and humans

About 34,000 years ago, one of our human ancestors sat and carved a tiny horse from a mammoth's tusk using a stone tool. This amazing carving (below) was only discovered in the 1930s! Horses and humans have a long, shared history.

Horses are still milked in remote areas of Asia.

The Vogelherd Horse, one of the earliest known works of art, is just 2½ in (4.8 cm) high. The carving probably originally had legs.

The first riders?

The Botai, hunters living in Central Asia, were almost certainly riding horses around 5,500 years ago, as well as milking them.

Horses enabled Native-American tribes to hunt over larger areas.

Into war

The invention of the horse-pulled chariot around 2,000 BCE opened the way for new forms of warfare. The invention of spoked wheels made chariots lighter.

THE TROJAN HORSE

This mythical wooden horse was taken into the besieged city of Troy in the belief that the invading force, the ancient Greeks, had left it behind. However, the horse was filled with Greek soldiers, who let their army into Troy to defeat the inhabitants and claim victory.

Learn more about Bucephalus on page 35.

An important step

A key development in horseback riding was the stirrup. It is thought that the first stirrup was used simply to make mounting a horse easier. Stirrups helped stability and that aided control, particularly in warfare.

A mighty team

One famous human-horse partnership was that of Alexander the Great (356–323 BCE) and his mighty horse Bucephalus.

Horses in North America

Horses had been extinct in North America for thousands of years before being reintroduced in the 1600s. They changed the lifestyle of thousands of Native-American tribes, such as the Sioux and Cheyenne.

Jousting

Knights were important people in Medieval Europe. Riding into battle on warhorses, they fought for kings and nobles, helping to defend their castles or conquer new lands and peoples.

Terrible tournaments

The earliest jousting tournaments started as a mêlée. Teams of mounted knights fought violent mock battles with all kinds of weapons—swords, axes, spears, maces, and flails. Ouch!

The armor for rider and horse weighed about 130 lb (62 kg).

A lance was traditionally made of wood with a metal tip.

A shaffron protected the horse's head.

The knight slotted into a saddle that had a high back and front.

Full protection

Not only the knights but also their horses needed protection from lethal weapons and high-speed collisions. Full horse armor, known as a bard, was rare because it was expensive and required a heavy horse to support it.

The metal armor was lined with padded fabric.

Colored plumes identify the knight.

Charge!

At peacetime, knights trained hard at riding and fighting, and showed off their skills at contests called tournaments. The joust was the main event. Two knights charged at each other to try and knock the other knight off his horse with a long weapon called a lance.

In today's reenactments, each rider aims the lance at the other's shield.

A knight's horse

A rich knight would have different types of horse:

● A strong destrier was used for battle charges.

● A rouncey was favored for swift raids and pursuits.

● A palfrey, a small horse, was used for riding and hunting.

Heavy work

Horses have been used to transport people and their goods from one place to another for thousands of years. In fact, until the beginning of the last century, the world's economy was largely dependent on horsepower.

On the farm
Since ancient times, horses have pulled heavy plows across fields to turn the soil and make it ready for planting. However, horse-drawn plows are now rarely seen.

The term used to measure the pulling power of an engine is still called "horsepower"!

On the water
During the 1700s and 1800s, horses towed long, narrow, flat-bottomed boats called barges beside rivers and canals in Northern Europe.

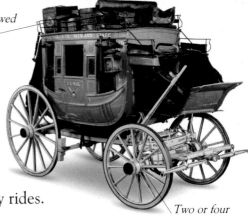

On the road

Horse-drawn stagecoaches were common before road and rail transportation; they made for long, bumpy rides.

Luggage was stowed on the roof.

Two or four horses were hitched to the front.

Going underground

In England in the 1800s and 1900s, ponies were used for work in coal mines. They were usually well cared for, but rarely came above ground.

Horsepowered

The Industrial Revolution that began in England 250 years ago brought in all kinds of new machines, but it would not have happened without the horse. This machine used a horse to grind corn to make flour.

Giant wheel

This horse is turning a mill wheel to grind corn.

Shaft attached to grinding stone.

Pony Express

This mail service ran for just 18 months in 1860, with riders changing galloping mounts frequently to carry mail an amazing 2,000 miles (3,200 km) across the US.

Still going strong

Much of the heavy work that horses have traditionally done is now done by machines. But horses are still used for certain kinds of transportation, and for plenty of other specialized tasks.

Pack it on
Pack horses and donkeys still carry people and goods in areas where there are no roads for cars and trucks, or where people are too poor to own a vehicle.

Law and order
Mounted police are a familiar sight in many countries. The first mounted police were London's Bow Street Horse Patrol, formed in England in 1758. Police horses are well trained.

Search and rescue
When people get lost in wildernesses too remote to search by foot, riders may sometimes comb the area while helicopters look from the air.

Mongolian children race their horses at the Naadam, a popular festival. Each race is up to 18 miles (30 km) in length.

Land of the horse

The nomads that wander central Asia's vast prairies rely on tough horses for many tasks. In Mongolia, a horse's skill is celebrated at an annual summer festival.

The rider controls the horse with his feet.

Each kettle drum is solid silver and weighs 90 lbs (40 kg).

Ceremonial horses

Horses appear in festivals and ceremonies in many parts of the world. Drum horses such as this one have to be powerful but even-tempered.

Horses have been used to round up cattle for hundreds of years.

Ranch life

On large farms or ranches, horses are sometimes still used to herd cattle. They move along with the cattle easily, making sure the herd stays together and that no animal is lost.

Feathers hide the hooves.

Early horses

About 60 million years ago, a timid four-legged mammal, no bigger than a hare, browsed the forests of North America. Paleontologists believe this creature, the Dawn Horse, was an ancestor of the horses we see today (in addition to being related to tapirs and rhinoceroses!).

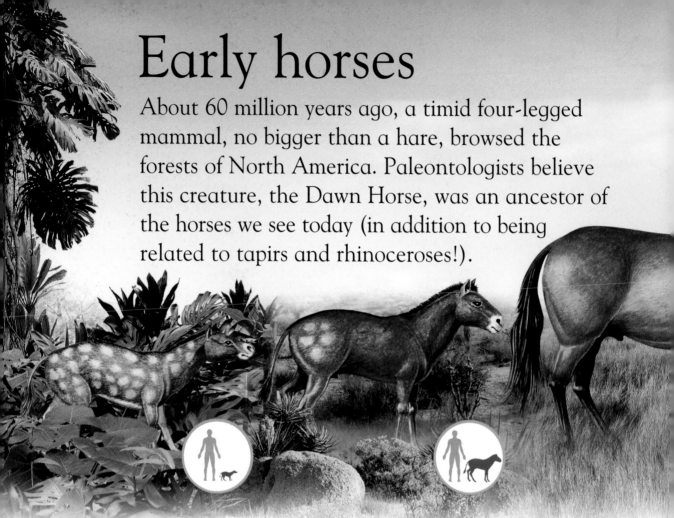

Dawn horse

Hyracotherium, the Dawn Horse, could be found in North America 50 million years ago (mya). Small teeth show it was a browser, probably favoring soft leaves and fruit.

Middle horse

Looking back 40 million years sees the emergence of *Mesohippus*, slightly larger than the Dawn Horse, at about the size of a sheep. This animal wandered in a more open landscape, with fewer forests.

Hoof development

As the horse's environment changed, so did its toes, evolving from multi-toes encased in fleshy pads to a single toe protected by a hoof. This change happened gradually, over the course of millions of years.

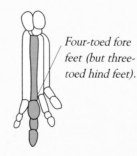

Four-toed fore feet (but three-toed hind feet).

HYRACOTHERIUM
moved on soft, moist soil, the spread of the toes preventing it from sinking.

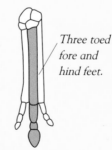

Three toed fore and hind feet.

MESOHIPPUS
rested its weight on its middle toes, but still walked on three toes.

Single, strong center toe.

PLIOHIPPUS
was the first one-toed horse. The toe was protected by a hoof.

These are four stages in the development of Equus.

One-toed horse

This creature, *Pliohippus*, was about the size of a donkey and lived between five and 10 mya. It had longer, stronger teeth, to cope with the tougher vegetation of a drier climate. It probably roamed open plains.

Equus

A more recognizable ancestor of today's horses appeared around four mya. *Equus* was the size of a pony, and, with its longer legs, an adept runner over the larger areas of grassland that had changed the landscape.

Reaching new places

Equus emerged in North America, so how did its descendents spread? They migrated via Ice Age land bridges. When the ice receded (about 10,000 years ago), the horse disappeared in North America. No one knows why. It was reintroduced in the 1600s.

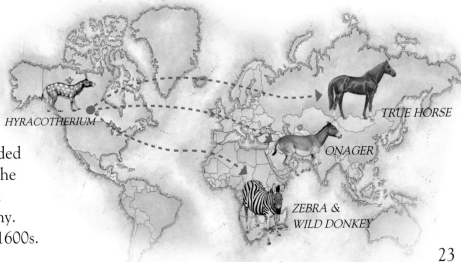

HYRACOTHERIUM

TRUE HORSE

ONAGER

ZEBRA & WILD DONKEY

23

Wild horses

Horses ran wild for thousands of years before being tamed by humans. There are now no wild horses, although some experts think the Przewalski's horse—a primitive horse that survives today—is related to these early breeds.

Wild origins

Also known as the Asian wild horse, Przewalski's horse has been extinct in the wild since the 1960s, but groups are gradually being reintroduced from small captive herds.

One big family

Equidae, the horse family, includes four types of horse— Przewalski's horse, domestic horses (including ponies), wild donkeys, and zebras.

PRZEWALSKI'S HORSE These horses have short manes and no forelock.

DONKEYS There are three types of wild donkey: the African wild donkey, kiang (left), and onager.

ZEBRA This is the one truly wild member of the horse family.

The African wild donkey is one of the world's rarest mammals.

The African wild donkey has legs striped like a zebra.

A true survivor

Like its wild ancestors, an African wild donkey is tough. It can survive for two or three days without water, living on almost any plant material.

It's just a zebra!

You may think that all zebras are alike, but, that's not the case: there are three species of zebra and each species has a different pattern to its stripes. In fact, no two zebras have the same pattern of stripes (just as no two humans have the same fingerprints).

GREVY'S ZEBRA
The largest of the zebra family.

PLAINS ZEBRA
The most common of all zebras.

MOUNTAIN ZEBRA
Has a fold of skin, called a dewlap, on its throat.

Mix them up!

● A zebra crossed with a donkey produces a zedonk.

● Crossing a male donkey and a female horse produces a mule.

● A male horse and female donkey produce a hinny.

● A horse and zebra produce a zorse.

Can a zebra be tamed?

Zebras have not been successfully trained to work for humans except in a few cases. That's because they tend to get aggressive as they get older and they panic easily.

Zebras are rarely used in this way, since their reactions can be unpredictable.

25

Feral horses

Herds of mustangs roam the Great Plains in the American West. These are feral horses; the descendants of domestic horses. Feral horse herds can be found all over the world.

Conquistadors were Spanish explorers and conquerors who seized land in the Americas.

Route to America

Horses were first brought to North America by Spanish conquistadors about 400 years ago. Some escaped or were set free, and by 1900 there were about two million feral horses in the US. Mustangs were seen as pests and many were killed. They are now protected by law.

Who's the boss?

All horses prefer not to fight, but in a feral herd the dominant stallion will do so in order to maintain his position over a group of mares. Usually the weaker horse backs off pretty speedily

Feral horse facts

- There are an estimated 25,000 feral mustangs in 10 Western states of the US.

- About half of these mustangs are in Nevada.

- The Camargue is one of the world's oldest breeds, but was not officially recognized as a breed until the 1960s.

French feral herds

Sometimes referred to as "the horse of the sea," semiferal Camargue horses roam saltwater marshland in southeastern France. Adults are gray, but foals are colored brown or black and turn gray as they get older.

Route to Australia

Feral horses are known as "brumbies" in Australia and there are lots of them—far more than any other feral horse elsewhere. Horses first arrived in Australia in 1788 on the First Fleet, eleven ships that sailed to Australia from Great Britain. There were just seven of them. By 1850 they numbered 160,000 (due to breeding), and there are now some 400,000 feral horses in Australia.

Important breeds

Worldwide there are about 250 breeds of horse. Three of the most important breeds are the Arab, the Thoroughbred, and the Barb. Of these, the Arab and the Barb were the first to appear.

The amazing Arab

The Arab first appeared in Arabia and North Africa about 3,000 years ago. It is highly prized for its beauty, intelligence, and speed. Arab horses have 17 ribs—other breeds have 18.

Elegant head with dished face.

An Arab horse holds its tail high when moving.

Large nostrils

Colors are brown, bay, sorrel, black, or gray.

Horse facts

● Arab and Thoroughbred horses are called "hotbloods" because they are quick and athletic.

● "Coldbloods" are heavier horses, such as Clydesdales.

● All Thoroughbreds can be traced back to three stallions from the 1600s and 1700s.

King Solomon (the ruler of Israel from 972 to 922 BCE) is rumored to have had more than 40,000 Arab horses in his stable. Many were captured in battles.

The bold Barb

The Barb, a North African desert horse, is one of the toughest horses in the world. It has great stamina and can run very fast over short distances. Being a desert horse, it can bear high temperatures and little water. It is used for riding, racing, and jumping.

Born to run

The Thoroughbred is a race horse and is the fastest breed in the world. It originated in England in the seventeenth century.

The Barb is incredibly agile.

The hoof is usually fairly narrow, a trait shared with other desert horses.

Owning a horse

Do you dream of owning a horse? If so, you have a lot to consider. Horses need daily attention, and it's worth helping out at a local stable before committing to your own horse. Here are some of the basics you should know.

Good grooming

A horse needs to be kept clean, and grooming it daily will ensure that it is. Grooming is also useful for checking the condition of your horse, because you'll quickly spot any bumps or cuts. Horses enjoy being groomed.

It is better to groom a horse once it is tied with a headcollar and lead rope and before it has been tacked up.

Metal comb for cleaning brushes.

Hoof pick

A rubber curry comb is used to clean away dried mud.

This horse has a blanket clip.

The dandy brush is used for the body.

Sponges are used to clean the eyes, nostrils, and dock.

What will I need?

Each horse should have its own grooming kit, kept in a clean container that can be carried to the horse. Always store brushes with the bristles down—it helps the brushes to last longer.

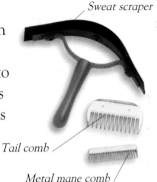

Sweat scraper

Tail comb

Metal mane comb

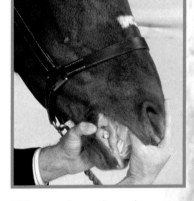

Frog

Hoof care

Hooves should be checked for stones. Use a hoof pick, and clean from the heel to the toe. Clean away from the central frog.

Time for the dentist

A problem with the teeth can cause a horse to become very bad-tempered. Regular dental checkups are a must.

Time for a haircut

Horses may need to be clipped if they are working hard or they can overheat. There are a number of different types of clip.

Tack care

A horse needs its tack professionally fitted, since poorly fitting tack can cause sores and hard skin. Clean a leather saddle and bridle regularly to keep the leather supple.

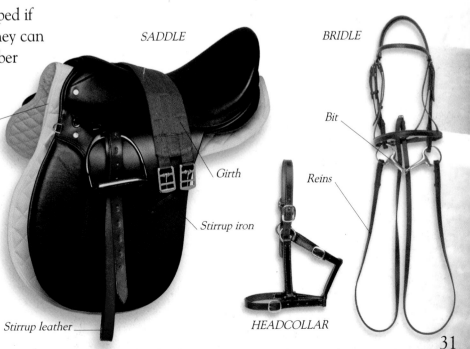

SADDLE

Numnah

Girth

Stirrup iron

Stirrup leather

BRIDLE

Bit

Reins

HEADCOLLAR

Looking after a horse

In addition to good grooming and tack care, a domestic horse has many other requirements, from its food to its field and shelter.

Live-in

Some horses live outside in a field with a shelter. Others are stabled. A stable needs to have a thick, clean bed. This may be straw, wood shavings, shredded newspaper, or hemp.

Corn

Oats

Barley

Hay

A saltlick supplies a horse with salt as and when it's needed.

Apple

A horse drinks about 10 gallons (38 liters) of water per day.

Time for dinner

An active horse requires certain foods in addition to grass and hay to keep its energy levels high. Many horses receive compound foods, which are mixes of food types.

Cleaning up

Stables have to be mucked out at least twice daily, because horses can pick up infections from a dirty stable. Dung must be removed from the bedding, which in this case is straw, and fresh bedding put down.

Space

Horses need a lot of space in which to live and move around. Ideally, a horse needs an area the size of a football field to supply it with the exercise and grazing it requires.

Keeping company

Horses are herd animals and crave company. If it's not possible to keep more than one horse, it's a good idea to introduce another companion.

Horse whispering

Horse whispering is all about learning to communicate with a horse by first understanding why horses act the way they do. Its use dates back at least to 350 BCE, when a Greek writer, Xenophon, wrote *On Horsemanship*.

Xenophon was a Greek soldier and writer who suggested the use of a more thoughtful approach to horses.

Horse whispering is about mimicking natural techniques.

Body language

Most human communication is nonverbal. Your body language talks, and it talks loudly to a horse. How you present yourself, where you look, how big or small you seem, and your tone of voice are important.

First steps

For a horse to respond well to a trainer, it has to get used to being handled. It's best to do this from a foal's first year. How a foal is handled will have an effect on how it will behave when fully grown.

Behave!

A foal is disciplined with a quick nip. The foal learns to behave, because it wants the mare's protection. Some horse trainers build on this instinctive behavior, encouraging through frequent praise and reward.

AN EARLY HORSE WHISPERER

The story goes that some 2,300 years ago, 12-year-old Alexander the Great tamed the powerful black stallion Bucephalus by recognizing that the horse was afraid of its own shadow, and so turning it to face the Sun. His father gave him the mighty horse as a reward.

Gaining trust

Once a horse trusts its trainer, it will face all kinds of unexpected things, as shown by this horse's relaxed reaction to a large ball.

Follow the leader

Horse whispering depends on the recognition that horses crave companionship and protection. Most horses want to follow and not lead. If they believe a person is a safe leader, they will follow.

35

Horse riding

Good riding schools can be found all over the world and many children take riding lessons. Whether you take a lesson or a ride in the country, there's a lot of fun to be had.

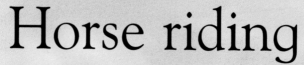

Riding hat

Gloves

Riding whip

Jodphurs

Riding boots

What will I need?

A rider needs safe and comfortable clothing. Jodphurs or leggings are good because they stretch. They also keep your legs from rubbing against the stirrup leathers. Always wear strong boots with a small heel and a hard hat.

This is a flash noseband. It has two straps, one passing under the bit.

There are many different bits. Not all horses will need a bit as strong as this one.

Riding schools

- Visit your local riding schools if you can rather than booking a first lesson by telephone. Check around!

- Do the horses look healthy and alert? Are the stables clean and in good repair?

- Ask if you can watch a lesson take place, and see if you like the teacher.

On the lunge

For your first few lessons, your pony will be led by someone on a lead rope. It's also good, later on, to have a few lessons on a long lunge rein. On the lunge rein, while your teacher controls the horse, you can concentrate on finding your balance in the saddle.

Going up... coming down

Always mount and dismount from the left-hand side of a horse and ask someone to hold the horse. There are different ways to dismount. One method is to take both feet out of the stirrups and swing your right leg over the back of the horse, then spring down.

Sit up! Relax!

As you learn to ride, your teacher will suggest ways of using your legs, or using your weight. Learning to use aids—legs, hands, voice, and body weight—is an important step toward becoming a more experienced rider.

Hands should be level.

Sit tall, but always stay relaxed.

The reins should not be tight or hang in loops.

Push heels down and use the balls of the feet in the stirrup.

At a glance: first steps

Once you have mounted, you have to check that your stirrups are the correct length. Your instructor will help you learn how to adjust them yourself.

To start walking: look ahead and close both legs gently against the horse's sides. Some horses will respond to the command "walk on."

To turn: look where you want to go, then position your weight. To turn left, squeeze gently on the left rein and also the left leg. Allow the right rein to slacken slightly so the horse's head can turn.

Riding styles

English or Western? Horses are ridden in one of two very different ways. The English style is more formal, while Western riding developed in parts of the world where horses are traditionally used to herd cattle.

Large brimmed hat

Loose reins
Western reins are held loosely in one hand and the horse is steered by laying them against the neck. It's called neck reining.

Comfort riding
Western riding was developed by cowboys, who needed a comfortable means of spending long hours in the saddle. The horse is controlled largely by the rider's weight. The leg is pushed forward.

No noseband

Cantle

Pommel

Western saddle
Used for Western riding, these saddles are used on working horses on cattle ranches throughout the United States.

Fender

Leather stirrup

What kind of horse?
All horses can be trained to respond to Western Riding, but the most popular in use in North America is the American Quarter Horse.

Artificial aids, such as a whip, are sometimes used.

Protective hard hat

A constant touch

English riding achieves steering by increased pressure on the left or right rein and a lessening of pressure on the opposing rein, together with leg movements.

358

Noseband

Contact is maintained with the horse via the bit.

Cantle

Pommel

English saddle

English riding is not limited to English-speaking countries. This saddle type is used for many international equestrian competitions.

Stirrup iron

Walk on!

English riding sees the horse controlled largely by the seat, hands, and legs. The style is a formal method, with the leg against the side of the horse.

39

The main event

One of the most demanding of all horse sports is eventing. Competitors have to train for three types of riding: dressage, show jumping, and cross-country. It's tough and both horse and rider have to be at the peak of their fitness.

Cross-country tests the horse and rider's strength, fitness, balance, control—and courage!

A cross-country test

The most grueling part of eventing is the cross-country course. As competitors gallop through woods and fields, they face obstacles such as fallen tree trunks, ponds, steep banks, and wooden fences.

Fit to compete?

In a three-day event, a vet will inspect the horses before the start and at least once during the event to ensure they are fit enough to continue. This is called a "horse inspection."

Dressage

Dressage sees the horse and rider perform controlled movements in an arena, almost as if they were dancing. The smooth and graceful moves test the obedience and flexibility of an incredibly powerful horse.

A dressage rider must sit well on the horse and have it under perfect control.

Eventing facts

● The word "dressage" comes from the French word "dresser," meaning "to train."

● Eventing started in the Olympic Games in 1912, but only male cavalry officers were allowed to compete until 1952.

Hidden commands

Dressage aids can be difficult to spot, unless you know what to look for. The rider trains the horse to respond to the lightest touch of leg, seat, or hand.

On to the jumps!

Show jumping takes place in an arena. As a part of eventing, it has one round with 10 or 12 jumps. At the higher levels of competition, it usually comes last, so the horses are tired. The judges want to see if each horse has enough stamina to complete the competition.

A day at the races

From chariot races at the Colosseum in ancient Rome to steeplechasing today, the thrill of horse racing has attracted huge crowds for thousands of years. Racing demonstrates the full power and speed of a horse at the peak of its fitness.

Chariot racing
War chariots were first raced at funeral games in memory of heroes and kings of ancient Greece.

Flat racing tests speed, skill, and strength.

And they're off!
Flat racing is all about speed. It takes place on flat ground, with no obstacles, and is an internationally popular event that depends on the Thoroughbred. Flat race jockeys have to be light in weight, and are, therefore, usually shorter than jump jockeys who ride in steeplechases.

AND THE WINNER IS...
The Roman emperor Nero took part in a chariot race at the Olympic Games in 67 CE. However, the other chariots had four horses, while his had 10. When he fell out of his chariot, the other teams waited for him to get back in and let him win. They were scared of him!

Harness racing

This type of racing is popular in the US, Europe, Australia, and New Zealand. A horse pulls a two-wheeled cart called a sulky, and this is where a driver sits. The horses run at a fixed gait, which can be a trot or a pace.

Steeplechase

The steeplechase began in Ireland in 1752 as a cross-country race between two friends over fields, hedges, and gates to a steeple-topped church. England's Grand National is the most famous and difficult steeplechase in the world, with a staggering 30 jumps.

Today's racing jockeys wear distinctive colors, so they are easy to identify. These are called "racing silks."

Horse games

Horses have helped human beings in so many ways over the centuries. But horses and humans also have fun together through different sports and games.

Roman riding dates back almost 2,000 years. A rider stands with each foot on a different horse.

The game of kings

Polo is like playing field hockey, but on a horse. Each team of four players has to hit a ball into the other team's goal to win a point. The match is played in short rounds called chukkas.

For my next trick...

Trick riding sees a rider performing fabulous stunts, usually on a galloping horse or horses. Stunts like this take years of training to perfect.

The word polo comes from the Tibetan word "pulu," which means "a ball."

Helmet

Knee guard

Polo mallet

Whip

Bandage for protection.

Polo ball

Show jumping

Barrel racing

Bending race

Fun and games

Many children, and adults as well, enjoy equestrian gymkhana games—racing against opponents on short obstacle courses that test their riding skills and stamina. From barrel racing to the bending race, these games are fast and fun.

Best in show

Rosettes are common at many horse shows, awarded for best of breed and turnout or to the winning horse and rider in a gymkhana event. Award colors vary from country to country.

Buck up!

Popular in North America, rodeo is a sport that tests the skills of a cowboy, and dates back to the nineteenth century. Events include saddle-bronc riding, bareback riding, bull riding, steer wrestling, calf roping, and team roping. Some countries ban rodeo events.

Glossary

Here are the meanings of some words
it is useful to know when learning about horses.

aid The means by which a rider communicates with a horse, using, for example, weight, legs, voice, and hands.

bit The part of a bridle that fits into a horse's mouth.

bridle The tack a horse wears on its head.

coldblood A name used to describe heavy horse breeds such as the Jutland and Shire.

colt A young male horse.

conformation The shape of a horse or pony. Good conformation means a horse is well proportioned.

dressage A method of improving a horse's obedience. It consists of carefully controlled movements that demonstrate the balance and agility of a horse and rider.

eventing A competition that includes cross-country, show jumping, and dressage.

farrier A person who shoes horses.

feral An animal descended from domestic ancestors, but which now lives in the wild with limited or no human intervention.

filly A young female horse.

flat racing A type of horse race that is carried out on a flat course with no jumps or obstacles.

flehman A curling of the top lip that allows a horse to taste the air around it.

foal A horse that is under one year of age.

forelock The hair that grows on a horse's forehead.

gait The pattern of a horse's leg movements. All horses can walk, trot, canter, and gallop.

girth The measurement around a horse's body where the girth holds the saddle. Also the name of the strap that holds the saddle in place.

gymkhana Competitive games between teams of riders and horses.

hack A ride in the open and not in a school.

hand A unit of measurement for horses. It is used to describe a horse's height at its withers. One hand is 4 in (10 cm).

hinny A cross between a male horse and a female donkey.

hoof The hard part of a horse's foot.

horsepower A unit of power that measures the pulling power of an engine.

hotblood A Thoroughbred, Barb, or Arab horse, or one largely descended from these.

jodphurs Special riding pants.

lungeing A means of exercising a horse from the ground, using a long rein. The horse moves in a circle around the trainer.

mane The hair that grows on the back of a horse's neck.

mare A female horse that is more than four years old.

mule A cross between a male donkey and a female horse. Males cannot reproduce, but some females can.

points The external parts of a horse, such as its poll, withers, and chestnut.

pony A horse that is less than 14.2 hands high.

reins These attach to a bridle and are used in control a horse.

rodeo A competition popular in North America in which cowboys demonstrate skills that are related to riding and handling cattle.

saddle A piece of tack that the horse wears on its back.

stallion A male horse, used for breeding.

steeplechase Thoroughbred race traditionally across fields over fences and ditches, but now often held over a race course.

stirrups These are used to support the rider's feet and hang from the saddle.

tack Name for the equipment used for riding, such as a saddle and bridle.

warmblood A horse such as the Hanoverian whose ancestry includes hotbloods and coldbloods, .

withers The top of a horse's shoulders.

zedonk A cross between a zebra and a donkey

zorse A cross between a horse and a zebra.

Index

Acknowledgments

Dorling Kindersley would like to thank:
Andy Cooke for his original illustrations; Saloni Talwar, Camilla Hallinan, Dawn Henderson, Rukmini Chawla, Lorrie Mack, and Fleur Star for their editorial input; Pamela Shiels for design assistance.

Picture credits

The publisher would like to thank the following for their kind permission to reproduce their photographs: (a=above; c=center; b=below/bottom; f=far; l=left; r=right; t=top)

1 naturepl.com: Carol Walker. 2 Corbis: John Wilkes Studio (tl). 2-3 Photolibrary: Morales (r). 4-5 Photolibrary: Best View Stock (Background); Juniors Bildarchiv (fcrb); tbkmedia.de (crb). 5 Alamy Images: Juniors Bildarchiv (fcrb); tbkmedia.de (crb). Dorling Kindersley: The Natural History Museum, London (tr). 7 Photolibrary: Radius Images (r). 8 Getty Images: Photonica/Emmerich-Webb. 8-9 Photolibrary: Juniors Bildarchiv. 9 Alamy Images: Manfred Grebler (tr) (cr). 10 Photolibrary: Glyn Thomas (tr). 10-11 Sanjay Austa: (t/Background). Bob Langrish: (bc). 11 Photolibrary: Juniors Bildarchiv (tl) (cr). 12 Alamy Images: Juniors Bildarchiv (cl). Photolibrary: Jacque Denzer Parker/ Index Stock Imagery RF (bl). 12-13 Sanjay Austa: (t/Background). Getty Images: Stockbyte (bc). 13 Alamy Images: tbkmedia.de (crb). Photolibrary: Ingram Publishing RF (tl). 14 Corbis: Dean Conger (cra); Roger Wood (clb). Tuebingen University: Hilde Jensen (ca). 14-15 Corbis: Brian A. Vikander (br). 15 Corbis: Rolf Richardson/ Robert Harding World Imagery (tl). Dorling Kindersley: Pegasus Stables, Newmarket (tr). 16 Alamy Images: David Young-Wolff (bl). Corbis: The Art Archive (ca). 17 Photolibrary: Stephan Goerlich. 18 Corbis: Patrick Ward/Documentary Value. 18-19 Photolibrary: Sven Rosenhall/Nordic Photos. 19 Corbis: Bettmann (cr); Walter Bibikow/Encyclopedia (crb); Ed Young/Encyclopedia (tr); Photolibrary: (tl). 20 Alamy Images: SUNNYphotography.com (bl). Corbis: Macduff Everton (t). Getty Images: Joe Raedle (br). 21 Photolibrary: Alberto Campanile (b); Colin Monteath (tl). 22 Getty Images: Digital Vision (cla); Thomas Northcut (c/ Foliage background); Ron and Patty Thomas (cl) (cb); Erik Von Weber (cr/Foliage background). 22-23 Sanjay Austa: (t/Background). Getty Images: Joseph Sohm-Visions of America (c). 23 Getty Images: Comstock (tr); De Agostini (clb) (crb); Jennifer Thermes (br); Jeremy Walker (cr). 24 Alamy Images: tbkmedia.de (cl). Corbis: Steve Kaufman (bc). Getty Images: Art Wolfe (tr). Photolibrary: Barbara Von Hoffmann (cla). 24-25 FLPA: ImageBroker (cr). 25 Alamy Images: Mary Evans Picture Library (br). 26 Corbis: Bettmann (cl). 26-27 Getty Images: Eastcott Momatiuk (cl). 27 Corbis: Chris Hellier (tr). Getty Images: The Bridgeman Art Library/Thomas Baines (bl). 28 Photolibrary: Juniors Bildarchiv (bl); David Taylor-Bramley (cla). 28-29 Corbis: William Manning (tc). Photolibrary: Juniors Bildarchiv (c). 29 Getty Images: Ariadne Van Zandbergen (cra). Photolibrary: Juniors Bildarchiv (br). 30 Photolibrary: Pixland. 31 Alamy Images: Alexander Frolov (cl). Photolibrary: Austrophoto (ca). 32 Alamy Images: allOver photography (tr); foodfolio (c) (cla) (cra); Lori Schmidt (clb). Corbis: Goodshoot (crb). Getty Images: ZenShui/ Sigrid Olsson (bl). Photolibrary: Michael Krabs (crb/Salt). 32-33 Corbis: David Frazier (Background). 33 Photolibrary: Juniors Bildarchiv (br). 34 Getty Images: George Shelley Productions (crb). Photolibrary: Michele Wassell (bl). 35 Alamy Images: blickwinkel /Lenz (cl); John Joannides (br). Photolibrary: EA. Janes (tl). 36 Getty Images: Emmerich-Webb. 38 Photolibrary: Morales (Cowboy). 39 Animal Photography: Sally Anne Thompson (cla). Dorling Kindersley: W&H Gidden Ltd (bl). Photolibrary: Grant Pritchard (English rider). 40 Photolibrary: Mike Hill (Rider). 41 Animal Photography: Sally Anne Thompson (c). Bob Langrish: (tl). Photolibrary: Creatas (b). 42 The Bridgeman Art Library: Czartoryski Museum, Cracow, Poland (tl). Corbis: Mark Goldman /Icon SMI (c). 43 Alamy Images: Tim Graham (cr). Corbis: Mark Goldman /Icon SMI (tr). Photolibrary: Alfred Schauhuber (br). 44 Photolibrary: Heinz Kühbauch (b); Mattes (tl). 45 Alamy Images: Convery 6month (tl); mattphoto (tr); Linda Richards (tc); Sunpix Travel (ca). Corbis: Shawn Frederick (bl). Photolibrary: Bob Trehearne (crb). 46-47 Photolibrary: TAO Images Limited. 48 Getty Images: Michael Melford.

Jacket images: *Front:* : Corbis: Thinkstock bc; Getty Images: Annie Katz bl; Al Petteway t; Keren Su br. *Back:* Getty Images: Eastcott Momatiuk

All other images © Dorling Kindersley
For further information see: www.dkimages.com